CHAOTIC G(

ISABELLE BAAFI

Chaotic Good

faber

First published in 2025
by Faber & Faber Ltd
The Bindery, 51 Hatton Garden
London EC1N 8HN

Typeset by Hamish Ironside
Printed in the UK by Martins the Printers

The right of Isabelle Baafi to be identified as author of this work has
been asserted in accordance with Section 77 of the Copyright,
Designs and Patents Act 1988

A CIP record for this book is available from the British Library

ISBN 978-0-571-39095-3

Printed and bound in the UK on FSC® certified paper in line with our continuing
commitment to ethical business practices, sustainability and the environment.
For further information see faber.co.uk/environmental-policy

Our authorised representative in the EU for product safety is
Easy Access System Europe, Mustamäe tee 50, 10621 Tallinn, Estonia
gpsr.requests@easproject.com

2 4 6 8 10 9 7 5 3 1

For my mother and all my mothers, grand- and great-

Contents

There are years that ask questions and years that answer.
– ZORA NEALE HURSTON

Hard, cold and cruel is a man
Who paid too much for what he got
   – 'Ain't No Way', performed by ARETHA FRANKLIN

SEPARATION

The Mpemba Effect

A phenomenon in which hot water freezes faster than cold water

A husband, a wife. Consumed by all we hungered for.
You, the dominant taste in every bite, and I came in raw,
I was humble. I learned the right things for the wrong reasons:
sweating over a pot for days, tasting myself in wilting leaves and
light soup: gizzard, liver, tomatoes, chilli.
I never hated anything so much. Not
you, the meal. I couldn't stand
anyone but you. Waking up each day to
the soft press of your lips on mine as you left. Seeking
abandonments sweet enough to crave.
There are
more species of apple than human taste buds with which to enjoy them.
Give me a portion that will not open my eyes. Give me more.
Not the food – us.
Nothing ever spoiled so fast.
By our seventh year we ate around the rot.

By our seventh year we ate around the rot.
Nothing ever spoiled so fast.
Not the food – us.
Give me a portion that will not open my eyes. Give me more,
more species of apple than human taste buds with which to enjoy them.
There are
abandonments sweet enough to crave:
the soft press of your lips on mine as you left; seeking
anyone but you. Waking up each day to
you, the meal I couldn't stand.
I never hated anything so much. Not
light soup: gizzard, liver, tomatoes, chilli.
Sweating over a pot for days, tasting myself in wilting leaves. And
I was humble, I learned the right things for the wrong reasons.
You, the dominant taste in every bite. And I came in raw.
A husband, a wife, consumed by all we hungered for.

The way you say *pen*

sounds like *pain*, as in
a pain obeys the hand that drives it.

If you want to sack a city, all you need
is some paper and a good pain.

Every day I lost a pain, but you
gave me another to take its place.

Aged six. Our first trip without Dad:
I etch fire into my legs with my mother's pain.

The mind steers the pain
as much as the pain shapes the mind.

What a luxury and a curse, to live and die
by the torrent of my pain.

Rainclouds surround the registry. Organza-veiled
and blister-footed, I am yours with the flick of a pain.

'Fill out in block capitals with black ink.' Some truths
are only valid when the right pain writes them.

To the woman sobbing into her phone on a park bench

'You have no idea what he's really like . . .' – April 2020

I write the poem to forget you. To study you.
To keep you safe. Whichever you can forgive.
With a metre that mocks your palpitations,
a slant rhyme placing *tomb* on top of *you*.
Because like you I have never been as perfect
as a first-born son in his mother's eyes. I too know
what it's like to mop a man's mouth with your sleeve.
I know the scabs you worry. You lie so well it becomes real,
and scorn the women who pray for a man like yours:
broad-smiled and many-faced, fork-tongued with
tangled eyebrows, steady hands. What even teeth he has.
And how exacting their bite.
He had a wisdom deep enough to stand in, and you did –
leaning on his shoulder as you stepped into your tomb.
Mangled, as only a man could make you.
No one knows it like me. How you curl into him
like a child and watch the world fall in love with his light.
How, some nights, you still wait for it to find you.
When he beckons, you approach on all fours.
When he shines on you, you scatter.

Path of Least Resilience

I grew up in a trench like this: spring blossom
dancing into the arms of wet cement.

The city had many afflictions: volcanoes,
posthumanism, a cloud that followed everyone

who laughed too long. Plus the pig at the edge of town
trapped in barbed wire, eaten alive for days.

Every friend I ever hated lived there,
and the man who made a bouquet

of all the syllables of my name.
He came in like a cough of pollen,

settling on my eyebrows, lodged beneath
my fingernails. The way a single sesame seed

bursts shoulders into hives. Imagine our life
like this: pigeons waving at us through dirty windows,

despair nestling between us like a comma.
Imagine us against the sound of bed slats breaking,

breaking. There is a graze in becoming what you
condemned. The friendships sink easily.

Every pet inherits the same name. You learn
to lower yourself into the tub before the water,

run it shame-hot to the rim. If you're honest,
you'll introduce yourself as the scar

of all the possible yous you displaced.
You will disdain the cement that hardens your steps.

You will injure the feet that carried you.
Every morning, we re-laid the road

to try and correct our mistake. Every pig
refused to die until our knives hit bone.

Mamlambo, Marooned

No one will risk the river.
The elders say she lurks beneath the surface,
awaiting her next kill.
The brain-sucker, sea-dweller –
head of horse and neck of fish and body of snake,
eyes gleaming green.
They say she was once a woman who went mad
when she found out she was barren.
They say her husband was a prophet who had visions
of the men she pulled into her.
They say she cut off her legs to escape his wrath
and sprouted fins.

I dream it differently – the day she washed ashore,
the ridges of her thoughts:

scrubbed smooth by oyster shells,
with a squid's tentacles for bangles, its ink for lipstick,
a scoop of sea foam to slick down my hair.
The first boy I came across gleamed bronze
and when he wrenched off my scales,
I said nothing. But I was wise.
I sniffed his hand before I let him ride me.

In the light of day, I kneel when I greet my husband.
I curse the creature with the other wives.
I spy oceans in them too. But at night
her inhale draws back the tide, and I hear it.
The water calls me. I wet my feet with spit.
I run my nails along the palisade bars
and the echo precedes the sound that made it.
The dream is a memory. My future slithers
into its mouth.

In the yard, a hen walks backwards
so as not to turn its back on me. Atavistic fowl.
Who am I to disappoint it? Atavistic, foul.
I enter the water on all fours,
tumbling-diving-sinking back to my riverbed,
more salty than sane.

And my sister wives
wearing selves too tight to swim in.
Why not release them from their bondage?
Snatching them from the river's edge
dragging them down down

               downdown
                        down

                  down

            down

              down

Sigma

Am I the only one who is trying to be a cat?
I ruckus without even trying. Jolt through storms.

           I gave everything
just to brush against your feet.

To twist against the fall
and not ask how.

I have nail dents in the places
where I was holding myself in. I told you

they were back dimples, knee wrinkles,
palm lines. I took ice from the tray you filled

and held it against my lover's ankle.
Don't judge.

A sink is the closest thing
I ever saw to a perfect wife.

I was not last, I was long-lasting.
Tell me you believe that's true.

I kept my appetites where I knew you'd never look.
Eye ribald. Aye, wretchedly. I rue.

Exit Interview

I've started ending phone calls like on TV –
quick and heartless. The goodbye is implied.
A *need* becomes a *needle* if we let it.

My mother always said,
If you reach a fork in the road, go right.
But what if the right path is not the right path?

The way out is steeper than the way in.
But when a road reveals itself out of nowhere, I take it.
I take the coarse road and I don't look back.

In truth, I leave the way my father left:
piece by piece. My favourite books
and sharpest cutlery in the room across town

that I told myself I had rented 'for my writing';
my wedding ring gathering dust on a shelf
next to the watch I kept trying to give away.

And the apps I hid from view, the friends
I never introduced him to. The dream in which I shut
a corridor of doors, one by one. Peace by peace.

I choose right. I choose what's right.
I choose left. I choose what's left. I am the one
who soils my sheets and the one who cleans them.

Notes on Modality

Let's redefine the word *good*. I have never given
blood, but I held a bird once until it died.
And a day is only as good as the questions it asks.

Yesterday was waterproof. I wrote nothing.
I can't tell you who I was back then.

On the Ridgeway, I walk till dusk,
my fingers bloodless. It is easy to feel nothing.
When seen through a snowstorm,
every summit could be a depression.
I drop my glove in a ditch, abandon it too.

I want to call you and ask who gets the moral high ground
but I can bear no answers. I become a tomb to seal them in.
Abrasive and wild like the limescale in your kettle.
I go inside and write it all.
The light-starved ground, the clumsiness of ice.

When Wiltshire folds in on itself, I believe it.
I follow suit. I have been missing since I was born.
The only water for miles is a frozen pond
with ducklings that shudder at my footsteps.
The only garden is a woman who has broken her body
for more horses than men.

She offers me a seat by her fire, but I choose snow.
Snow keeps tracks to remind us what we've done.

When I return to the poem it is much changed –
harsher. It won't answer to its name.
I omit much, but I cannot indulge it that.
I rein it tighter till it welts.

Some cruelties draw you in before you realise
what you've done,
like the cut that only hurts
once you know it's there.

One side of a conversation with the bailiff at my door

A: That depends on your definition of value.

A: The rule was that whatever we could not afford we had to forge.

A: Yes, we got by.

A: Not exactly. Replace 'build' with *burn*, 'bribe' with *bride*, and 'bowl' with *box*. That's how.

A: I paid off the debt with a stone that I knew to be worthless. The man I gave it to was certain it was priceless. I still can't tell who scammed who.

A: If by 'own' you mean endure – everything.

A: Owning and loving have the same texture. Only the shoulder scraped smooth by their touch can tell them apart.

A: Between loving and losing? They always felt the same to me.

A: Loyalty, I suppose. That was the only trading chip I had.

A: Everyone who wanted it. Anyone who asked.

A: I mean, it's just basic supply and demand. It was nothing until it was his.

A: Sell it? No, no, I thought that would cheapen it. I gave it and gave it and gave it, and I don't know who has it now, but I imagine it's their favourite footstool.

A: No, he was the servant, I was the shovel. My finest talents are still buried.

A: That was the only parable where a man loved more desperately than God.

A: Who else could he have owed? I'm the only one who made an altar of his words.

A: I don't know her name.

A: Sometimes, raindrops on the window would reach out for each other on the way down. On those days, I knew.

A: Every day, she and I would go to the same shop, bring the same number of coins. She always got twice as much with hers.

A: No. I was never taught to haggle.

Janus

The two of us kept swapping faces.
By that point, it was the only thing keeping us together.
Buttercups turned when I passed as though I were you
and not just the face I wore
but also the name it answered to.

Why would you give me your name?
I can incriminate you with so much less.
I have a scab shaped like your foot,
the curves of my ear moulded to your voice.
And I made you too – being for being.
Your dreams are the sequels of mine
and the brown of your eyes is the earth I gave you.

One morning after a swap, someone asked me
your name, and I couldn't remember it –
but they were staring and you were staring
and smiling at me so sweetly. I started coughing
to fill the silence but I coughed so much
that everyone thought I was dying,
and now I'm tubed up in a forgotten room
with a number for a name and our faces
are stuck and no one will touch me.

I find a stranger's mirror in your pocket,
but I can't bring your self to look at it.
I am scared of what you might see.
I'm scared that if I were lost in a crowd,
it would still be your face I was looking for.

CHILDHOOD

The Kuleshov Effect

A phenomenon in which the meaning of an image is inferred
through the interaction of two or more sequential images

Am I good because I smile or because I make no noise when I do?

Am I good because I obey or because I make no noise when I do?

Am I good because I bleed or because I make no noise when I do?

Am I good because I pray or because I make no noise when I do?

Am I good because I break or because I make no noise when I do?

Am I good because I hide or because I make no noise when I do?

Am I good because I cry or because I make no noise when I do?

The Scarecrow

If I turn away from light, head bowed from the sun's
admonishing glare, and peel off from this crucifying wood,
this soil punished by a plough's claw;

if I stalk the village shadows, past the schoolhouse,
through the mire, ascending walls like ivy,
dodging moonglow and priests' flambeaux;

if I wrestle with the dark, obey the adder
wrapped around my wrist, dance with spirits in the graveyard,
stain my lips with the menses of a witch;

if I succumb to the pull of a milkmaid's braid, the trembling
of a rabbit underfoot, the frailty of fontanelle,
the softness of a child locked and wailing in a basement;

if I catch a rag doll by the dress, tear its seams,
hold it face down in a pail, pile its hair in the gut of a
wheelbarrow, shove its innards down the gullet of a well;

if I conjure a murmuration in the figure
of a scythe, and taunt the crows
who rule the sky but peck at dirt to cling to life;

will you adorn me with dandelions, paint my cheeks
with mulberry blood?

Will you offer up the bones of your dead when the straw
in your barns catches fire?

Will you give to me your withered grass, your grain
that refuses to bud?

Will you still say that I know nothing of you?
Will you still say that I am not a man?

Watermelon

a shapeshifter sleeps   in my brother's room   shape of a boot   then a wolf
then a mangled tree   he had a ball   it changed colour   when squeezed   he
taught the sun   to look away   when he went out   to hunt   i used to watch
him   through the bars of the safety gate   cutting watermelons   into smiles
i couldn't read   but in the scratches on his back   i saw every girl   he'd ever
wanted   when he finally let me in   i held the watermelon down   so it couldn't
roll away   and he gave me   the biggest smile of them all   the biggest smile
i had ever seen

Turkish Delight

i know   everything   how blood finds its way   in the dark   why earth spins
but never gets dizzy   which grown-ups are safe   to smile at   a wink means
they dream about you   a nosebleed means   you told a lie   once you learn a
word   you see it everywhere   *dirty*   is everywhere   but only you see it
a secret is a kind of forgetting   like a taste you have to unlearn   every time
like the tickles   that you pretend are bubbles   the sweetie   hiding in your
pocket   squeeze it tight   if it makes any noise   don't let it tell on you
remember to wipe the sugar on your mouth   before you go to bed   there are
ants watching by the door   waiting   to eat you in your sleep

Finding my dad in a can of baked beans

In supermarket aisles, you teach me to need, stacking cans
up to my chin – baked beans, corned beef,
carrots, peas. I heave our trolley against the weight
of a fear you have never unlearned.

At night, your prodigal car lights creep across my bedroom wall,
and I add you to my list of things that come to us tightly sealed.
On school runs, I plant tiny feet in the back of your driver's seat –
hoping you'll feel something.

Beanstalk-tall and paraffin-scarred:
Google Translate says your laugh means
    wandering echo
And me – your youngest bean. If I knew the way back, I'd bury

scoops of me for you to find: in the Bantustan, near your
mother's house, the chirp of grasshoppers saturating the bush.
In the tracks on sloping road, made by your father's dusty Navara.
In the belly of the mine that swallowed your brothers every night.

The first time I hear your language, it's in the song of a baked-beans ad.
White families rush through drizzly streets to huddle in kitchens,
fall into dining-room chairs. Uniformed, backpacked kids
drift home to the baritones of Ladysmith Black Mambazo.

You've played that song on the stereo. I don't know
the words. But you say it's about
wise men, who cross the world looking for home
in a man they have always hungered for.

At the table, I nudge beans around my plate, clustering stars;
trying to navigate the miles between us. At the window,
the sides of the curtains shine like the rim of a half-opened can.
In the pauses between ads we chew on silence.

The Redemption of Vanity

Who told me I was naked?

Inclement clouds
who ask my nose why it's running
if it did nothing wrong.
Schoolboys who cycle past my house
and laugh at my crayoned face.

This poem is a lie
                      waxing true. This poem
is where every accusation hardens to bone:
        that my mother birthed me in a ditch
and when I fell to the ground I took on its hue.
        That I'm marked by all the stolen toys
I have hidden beneath my bed.
        That the eyes of aspens saw me
teach my darkness to the night.

When a lie mutates, every thought adjacent to it
inherits its texture. Palms become
palimpsests. Personhood in bas-relief.
A child may in fact begin to believe
she was made to disappear.

Close your eyes and learn it: to see yourself
in a teacher's ink. The bottomless well,
the inescapable grammar. The scratch
of blame, soft as a quill.

Imagine you are me. Imagine
thinking that you could.

They told that mole it could be so much more
and now it won't stop growing.

Chiaroscuro

ask me   about my first crush   the sand my brother piled on me   till i couldn't
breathe   he gave me a hammer   i didn't use it   but   i took its power   son
rise   son threat   son drinks   the rain that pools   in collarbones   mother's
hands   raking my scalp   yesterday   i pressed her sponge to the lake   to
clean it   now the lake is gone   it is easier to lasso the moon   than to help your
father   lay down to die   but what if   the tomatoes never went bad   what
if splinters   are a warning to run   i once found a ransom note   in my ear
the face in the photo was mine   i pawned everything   went to the drop-off point
no one ever came   to set me free   give me a bed   with no crumbs in it
pluck the fishbones   from my throat   i forgot where i hid   the matches   and
after that   it was easier   just to live in the dark

ADOLESCENCE

The Bystander Effect

A phenomenon in which the greater the number of people present,
the less likely each person is to help someone in distress

Her options were the same as ours:

    (a)   rude gyal
    (b)   weirdo
    (c)   class clown
    (d)   sket

All of them chafed. All of us were ugly then.
And in order to speak of *us*, I must first fill my mouth
with blood. Conjure fire like the cigarettes
put out on our eyelids; the slurs parting our hair;

the teacher dropping his pen next to the vista up our skirts;
the neighbour whistling us over, the car window
rolled down, the flash of pink. Who knows why
mounds sprouted from our chests,

the places we once tickled now swarming with hair.
Inundated by first blood – the flood, the fathoms,
the undertow. Cornered by Liam from the year above
where the only way out was older.

But [redacted] leaning in, even into that same fire.
A fast girl, the older ones said. So fast that she was fifteen
two years before us. And the flamingo legs and the foxy hair.
The reason boys followed us hens after school to the Coop,

the playground where we slogged under the weight
of Lambrini-packed bags. Same spot where
a camera once winked through pricks of holly.
Where every brick became a dare.

Where we'd squat under the climbing frame,
or against the ecstasy of a rocking horse.
Every day, [redacted] went behind the shed
with Darryl/Owen/Marcus/Akil . . .

One of them would smile and beckon,
fingers still wet with the last girl.
And [redacted] always came back
with mud-stained elbows and bee-stung calves.

We should've noticed the bleeding cuticles.
How she held her wrist when her uncle called.
We never doubted that the marks on her neck
came from a beast any larger than a bee.

     (a)   rude gyal
     (b)   weirdo
     (c)   class clown
     (d)   sket

We were each other's mirrors. Shattered but sure.
The highest form of praise was a rumour started
in your name. And what we didn't make ourselves
we pored over, poured into.

We plugged its holes with our fingers
and never felt the poison seeping in.
Our thoughts bloomed in other girls' mouths.
No, she was no rude gyal, no weirdo, no class clown . . .

And no, we never laughed, and even when we did
she never heard us, and even when she heard us,
she didn't know why, and even when she knew why,
it didn't matter:

at the park, when we pierced daisy stems with our nails,
there were no screams, no petals bruised.
For hours those afternoons, pushing one into the other.
Then another. Then another.

Laughing at the merry-go-round that groaned
when we jerked it around.
The reckless of us piled on a swing,
riding it till it broke.

Ouroboros

The chatroom is a children's sandbox
pulsating with snakes. Every now
and then the graphics spasm, sparkles
flashing us. Messages poke out
from the hem of the screen.

Some thirsts should not be quenched.
But here, at least, my 14/f/ldn is everything.

I type him back to mine most days,
my school skirt flung across a chair,
the pleats lacklustre too, puzzling
algebraic all the ways I am divided:

if x is a secret camgirl, what is her value?
Does x even know who x is?
If she does, why doesn't she reveal herself?
Why is she *always* revealing herself?

My panties peeling off like scabs,
the flesh beneath still tender, pink,
naively soft in a world that chafes.

I can't not do this.
Hunger made me; carved me in its image:
hands with which to touch, touch,
and a tongue to taste, and a belly –
his – in which to bury myself.

Hunger made me do it: seasoning
my pubescent veal, my fatty flesh
and oil-brushed hips, my raw hide
marinated in red lace and violet glitter,

the skin around my eyebrows
sore and bumpy, freshly tweezed.

I once heard a woman say
An apple chooses where it falls but not who eats it.
But why would the apple care?
The only purpose of an apple is to be eaten.
And the body that doesn't eat
for long enough will eat itself. It learns
to gather strength from its self-destruction.

Swallow me and I'll fill you up
and imagine that fullness is mine.
Tell me to suck my thumb like a child,
and I'll tell you how I taste.

The final spasm fades. Eyes open.
She sees nakedness. Her own.
She covers herself, closes the chat.
But because of the delay, she's still there –
filling his screen like a doe in an unhinged jaw.

Even now, years later, I sometimes feel like
I'm being watched. I tell my friends.
They say it's the Holy Spirit.

Even now, sometimes, I google myself
and scroll through pages of headshots,
holiday smiles, achievements since,
my belly gnawing, wondering if this time
I'll see a picture of a girl who looks like me,
in my old room, on the same mattress
I wet when I was three, leaning against a wall
once coloured with crayon and rainbow stickers.
A girl as black and void as pupils,
wanting anything to enter, settling for light.

hotboxing

bashiir is the last to
come: air force ones
mud-black &
sinking wet through
mildew carpet.
outside the night
bleeds on,
flashing & blue.
but here,
in a b&b's back
room, with earwax
walls & dirty light,
dangling webs &
wallpaper collapsed
in a weary heap;
one street from
the cellblock where
mosadi slept last
week; four stops
from the flytrap
where omari was
deported; between
the pub & the job
centre; in the lee of
an underground
track, exposed &
whining whenever
it's railed –
here, we use a towel –
cloud-coloured,
cough-rough –
to seal the door;

soak it till it dives to
black; drench it
with the things that
we once stretched
on toes as children
to reach: the spit on
our mother's thumb
cleaning our cheeks.
the froth of our
father's beer. the blue
of our brothers' too-soon
breathless blood.
bashiir was
stopped & searched
on his way over.
forged papers score
his rectum; scar the
part no missile could
reach; deliver him
from feltham, where
the plague is serving
eight to ten for
a block of coke &
hakim's blood
on his shoes.
the union jack flies
from the neighbour's
window. clouds the
moon. colonises its
light. in solidarity
with shadow, we
eclipse ourselves;

harnessing the flames
we've swallowed,
& promised
a white to blacken,
a ream to burn.
bashiir crinkles blue
rizla & green bush
under my nose. tells
me to lick it. i do.
says i got hands for
rolling. i do.
we light up & the
papers curl back,
sneering. & we – six
on a bed, a block of
shame, each shade of
night – we dig into
each other, elbow
deep. jay shows me
the shell behind his
molar. the gulf
between his knuckles.
the cure behind his
fly. i breathe & this
old cloud remembers
you. knows the
weight that deflates
your chest. sighs the
ways you have tried
to fill yourself.
a comic watches us
through the tv.

jokes about a black hole
that looks like
our neighbourhood.
mosadi laughs; a
cluttered choke on
truths too hard to
swallow. we lick the
bitter film on our
lips. we pilgrim to
blue flame &
withered leaves.
we ready for our
door to be kicked in,
for ash to scatter.
we practice smiles the
papers wouldn't
print. we wield limbs
heavy as blocks &
dutty grind to forget
how hollow.
we are so cool we let it
burn our fingers, singe
our lips. we are so fly,
we spider ourselves
in twists of spit
that we pass round –
& when we taste
ourselves for what we
are, we blow & laugh.
our senses cloud.
the guys unzip,
unleashing the rank

warmth of boys &
bowels poking
through gashes
oozing untouched
girls boujie & black, a
gasping kind of easy,
powdered with blue
eyeshadow & bubble-
gum shellac. calling
back the mules to
count the papers in
their hooves, to
gather up the white
dust in their fur. too
buzzed to go back to
the tower block, the
estate downwind
from the sewage
plant, where the
refuse of the rest of
the world becomes
our drinking water.
in summer smell hot
shit, dead foxes, fly-
tipped trash from
uptown shops – at
least, so saith jay:
apothecary in the
corner – with
conspiracies of lizard
queens, & corporate
logos hid in clouds;

of cockroaches who
scour black bags for
ciphers. a motorbike
brings chicken, lamb,
gin, blue curaçao; the
oil so hot it sizzles,
the ceiling licked by
steam. we wet their
zoots until their
paper droops. we
splendour in their
grade-a grass & blow
into the parts that
they want numb.
someone blocks the
door & they
become our anchors
when we start to fly.
they twirl our baby
hairs with fingers,
hold them down
when they're too
drowsy to stand.
tomorrow, when other
girls finger our
edges, beg the same,
we'll say it costs the
price of an eighth,
& the firm patter of
rain from clouds
they'll blow over
their own heads.

P___Y

PATSY

call me lamb of god

 i too was called out amongst my people

 set apart

 set upon

 by my people

 i laid hands on a boy once and felt him rise

he used to crawl through my window at 2 a.m.

 wide-eyed and blood volcanic

 he hid grapes beneath his tongue

 he had a scar on his throat

 in the shape of a bee

 he was both the sting it wielded and the honey it made

 which one did i yield to

 which portent was most exact

a dead balloon from my seventh birthday

 the key my mother hid in a bag of flour

every hamster i buried alive

every hand that has worshipped inside my skirt

what do you call the first drop of rain on your cheek

what if i told you it had been aiming for you

i never learned to fear cul-de-sacs

not knowing the fists that curl in cul-de-sacs

i gave my passwords to every email that asked

embraced every raging wind

i ran through that crowd

towards that familiar scent

let it sear my cheek with a kiss

PARRY

A golden shovel after Caleb Femi's 'Concrete (IV)'

The first time my mother sold me for food i
was twelve, and i don't know whose van it was
but i know that he made sure it was warm, and the
back smelled like pork rinds and chicken marrow,
and so when he turned away i sucked the corner of
the rug, and listened to the girls skipping on concrete
outside – even though there was no song – and the marking
on his arm was his child's name with a rose (and she was my
age too), and she looked like him but laughter made the pain
as tiny as a pebble in my shoe – but even in a pebble there
is torment, and her face her father's face was mine, and so turning against
her felt natural, but still it's strange, punching the body you once embraced; its
flesh bursting like a plum, its seams betrayed by the softness of its texture.

PENNY

A good neighbour is
a twitching curtain, an ear pressed
to a shared wall.

When she was born, the
trees shook themselves until their blossom
filled the street.

Her aunts presented her with
two potatoes: one raw, one rotten.
She swallowed them both.

A calm street. She plays
alone. Doesn't see eyes peek
through letterboxes.

The first time, bored in
her room. She found bliss against
her teddy bear's chest.

We don't blame pavement
when it cracks. We know the roots
bursting from within.

An abandoned fawn
stumbling into every bush
that smells like her mam.

Why is a daughter
like a dishwasher? Which one
holds more of our filth?

A red bike concealed in
grass. Ashamed of how much it
wants to be ridden.

Even the house disapproved –
winds gasping through keyholes,
clocks tutting as she slept.

I could see it in her eyes,
the landslide. The way she gripped
the edge of my sofa for dear life.

July heat – friction
of laughter. Gaunt shadows
in the road rise like flames.

PUSHY

Don't trust them ones that won't look. We have to look.
We slip Deputy Head a tenth to skip detention.
Jade pings the mandem from Brum who say they'll come, say they
like the way girls roll around when they scrap.

We slip Deputy Head a tenth to skip detention.
Cleo's nose ring swapped for a stud and cornrows tight
like two girls rolling around when they scrap.
Already in her mouth the taste of blood.

Cleo's nose ring swapped for a stud and cornrows tight.
That bitch is done, she says, smacking gum against her lips.
Already in her mouth the taste of blood.
A taste is all she wants, we think. This one is all bark and no bite.

That bitch is done, she says, smacking gum against her lips,
pacing in front of P's house. Then Cleo calls her out, hugs her.
A taste is all she wants, we think. This one is all bark and no bite;
she never could hit harder than she loves.

Cleo pacing in front of P's house. She calls her out, hugs her.
Then shoves her back, smacks her down. And when P gets up,
somehow, Cleo hits her harder than she ever loved –
her rage dividing shoulder from socket, underwear from crotch.

She shoves her back, smacks her down – and when P gets up
we yell, cos we're supposed to. Because that's why we came.
Her rage dividing shoulder from socket, underwear from crotch.
We all know that if it wasn't P, it could easily have been us.

And we yell cos we're supposed to. Because that's why we came.
Our hands as rough as Cleo's, but nuttin a likkle cream won't fix.
We all know that if it wasn't P, it could easily have been us:
snapping at our heels the hate we've run from since we were born.

Our hands as rough as Cleo's but nuttin a likkle cream won't fix.
Does shame have a scent? Do we wear it well? The girl's pit bulls
snapping at our heels. A hate we've run from since we were born.
And we laugh over train tracks, bridges, tunnels, our echoes laughing back.

Does shame have a scent? Do we wear it well? The girl's pit bulls
bark in our dreams: *today it was her, but tomorrow it will be you.*
And we laugh over train tracks, bridges, tunnels, our echoes laughing back,
sprinting on wet pavement, hoping the puddles will make us clean.

PUTTY

He wakes before dawn – escaping dreams – a dead end – the shapes of dogs
A gallon of water – four egg yolks – five miles – run by the river – race the dogs

Clay knuckled into the form a man – rough elbows – ripped toenails – bruised eyes
Every night climbing out of his father's fists – the terror – the hatred of dogs

His mother's tears made the sugar clot – her handprint – still stains the front door
She left it unlocked – hoping one day he'd follow – escaping the place of dogs

What is a boy if not a brick – both to build and destroy – hardened by a fiery glare
His box of beaks torn off birds – chewing bones like his father – the trait of dogs

He slept in the sink once – prayed to be clean – washed the kennel with bare hands
When punished – his face was shoved in their mess – can't forget the taste of dogs

He wanted to be yeast when he grew up – he envied the way dough puffs its chest
He would eat his own hair – hiding self in self – ashamed of his face of dogs

At nine he was given a sister – he fed her plums – tied his hair around her wrist
And the part of him that was dead – grew back when he held her – the grace of dogs

As she grew – he could tell she was lonely – she rode a different stud every night
He would scour midnight alleys – tracking her scent – the desperate haste of dogs

On the day the mob comes – he wonders – how many of them have made her yelp
The bitches call her out and she goes – they pounce – the crush – the weight of dogs

His whole life has led him here – this chance to matter – this child to protect
But the world set its sights on her – the day she was born – the bait of dogs

His fists are too few – his feet too slow – he sends out a faster horde
The mutts he trained for years – taught his malice – nothing like the pace of dogs

His sister lies in the road – the dogs leap and snap – the crowd scatters and screams
What they deserve, he snarls – a pack hunting a pack – the chase of dogs

The mob will tire first – he knows – he could never outrun what hunted him either
Destiny has teeth – the road where she played now bloodied – the fate of dogs

PIGGY

worst thing about them is the smell
it   drenches everything   and we know
death   we have seen butchers
this is worse   bloodied and burning
riot   to survive   you should
stay ready   listen with your feet
in dogs' teeth   your future and past
brother dribbling in a football cage
sister trapped in a room with three boys
you look away like you planned it
cut zip ties with a mirror shard
never knew how fast you could run until
it was home chasing you   you got out
but did you deserve it   who taught you
the origin of sin   why is this hollow
your hiding place
the only place no one looks

do you know
why we stopped you   were you
in the vicinity of the attack
did you see it   why did you
run   remove your humanity please
have you seen more births or deaths
which one looked like you   we see your
seething   your thieving   your spiteful
had you seen her naked before
did you want to   how did you escape
what else are you not telling us
you were running for your life
as though your life matters
which rock matches
the shape of your fist   which grave is
most sacred   most desecrated   is it in
the hood you wear   the who you wear

47

Everything is going according to plane

In my pregnant mother's rind, I was perfect: my skin
                as soft as a cotton bull, my handstands
bamboo straight. She had no ideal about
                        the moths I would hide in my belly button,
                the blood clot she'd sulk from my nose, the door
        that would split my forehead omen.
        Made from soggy biscuit crumbs
                        and born at the peck of summer,
        I was rot the daughter she wanted – but
                I stayed. I would slip motes under her door, confessing
                        everything I did wile she slept. The spilled milk
        from a broken hug. The uncovered bread that went stare.
                There is a voice recording of me at nine,
                        begging time to stop gushing me forward. But this poem
                is me at my beast, I sweat.
        For the next ten limes, I won't use
                a single worm that rhymes with *bitch*.
        Won't talk about the winter I ate
        only apples and Diet Coke.
        For my next prick, I will
                        make this thirteen-year-old girl disappear.
                These thins I paper over:
                        my neighbour's fate when my skirt blew up.
        My farther
                        telling me to watch for a parcel
                he never sent. My fist time, in a chestnut grove –
        hope thudding to the ground.
                        Everyone is tall but me. Every memory
                is divisible by its ache. Like Tudor Rose at sixteen.
Acid spray and dagger gleam. The buoy
                holding the wound of the boy
        painting the pavement with his neck.

What else but to burn it away? The next night
clinging to a melody
          with my lighter in the hair.
                        Screaming
    to resist the void. Singeing in the dark.

Ahead Only

Add a dead bird to the list of things I never chose
to see. The traps in moss-green eyes. Claw marks
around the mouth of a cave. No one told me

about the weeping sap of trees. The hymens
besieged. I was not prepared for waking and
realising I was not the only one inside me.

Trying to make amends for every branch I snapped
with my swinging. Every bar of soap my nails
have scarred. Every goldfish I let starve.

There are no good guys here. The sweetness
of a coconut is only attained through its breaking.
The pearls that decorate your throat

are the oyster shells torn apart. And when
you travel for a month and return,
and your local shop no longer sells dates,

you will wonder how many date palms
were counting on you to scatter their seeds.
And when you walk home at night, and a vixen

hears your footsteps, panics, and runs
under the wheels of a car, you will walk
on your hands and knees in guilt, and bury her

in the holes in your teeth, where everything
you love rots. But each night, a motherless fox
will imagine your baby's foot in its jaw.

There is a chilblain for each morning.
In every blushing winter sky, embarrassed
by our barrenness. In the eagerness of bees

who wait in pockets to feel our touch.
In being six years old, and pretending
to sleep in your father's arms – already fearful

of the day you would be too big to carry.
But we hide bruises with the things we fool ourselves
into forgetting. Like the fact that when a bear

catches a salmon swimming upstream, we all
identify with the bear – reaping what sustains it –
not the hope muscling to its own end.

MARRIAGE

The Horizon Effect

A problem in computer gaming whereby the number of possible outcomes
that a program can predict is limited, meaning the program may make
a detrimental move because it cannot see its error

O first love,
blessed and cursed love, shelter me
under your heel. From this angle you look just like
my father. Forget me just as quick.
Bind me with a name strong enough to kill my own:
in your mother tongue it sounds like *traveller*.
Lead me from myself, to red clay hills
and equatorial heat, a prophetic sun, a repentant tide.
Same shore my people were taken from.
A promise to return. Not to see, but to unsee.
To believe only what you show me.
To turn my back on who I was, feel her warmth fade
like the setting sun. Wondering if the light we destroy
is brighter than the light still to come.

Anti-Hero

You said you saw me through the crowd
and imagined rummaging through my hair.

Said you heard my laugh through walls
and could tell my fillings were made of gold.

My pixels make your pixels spasm.
I'm still not sure why.

When you ask me my favourite colour,
I send an encrypted file

from a laptop with no password.
The file cannot be opened because there are problems with the contents.

The file was copied and pasted
from a traumatised motherboard.

But you eat the rice I burned so I'll know
I am not too hard to stomach. Asking to touch

the dry patch I leave on a bench after sitting
in the rain. Wanting me to confide that once

I followed a snail to its nest
and drowned its eggs because they looked happy.

Once, I climbed a bell tower
and burned the rope with a mirror and the sun.

You tell me that your first job was
installing peepholes that worked both ways.

But the locals chased the inventor out of town
when the streets became full of suspicious couples

staring at each other's eyeballs for days.
Sometimes, I think it's for password clues that you ask

who taught me to ride a bike.
Why I buy so much bubble wrap.

Where I was when the last po'ouli died.
How I calm a memory when it's plucked.

Sometimes, I scratch the mole on my scalp
that you found when you washed my hair.

The parts of me that I only know exist
because you saw them.

Burst me into song

although perhaps

                                    not a symphony

but a hum

perhaps aloe vera for ulcerated gums

                        and leaf shadows dappling our chests

perhaps the equinox

perhaps afrobeats

perhaps yams   perhaps

homeostasis

perhaps orange peel brightens dark   thoughts

and the scar on my face

gives a lecture

on beauty   perhaps you hand me a fig

and our fingers graze

          and we leave the roast chicken

to burn

perhaps the chivalry of autocorrect   the motherhood

of bleach

perhaps your dirty socks and my unread books

the paper cut   the sucked thumb   the blood

covenant

perhaps the alarm warns us

about us

perhaps

enough points for a free latte

perhaps vegan steak   zero waste

the book of john

perhaps three buses in a row

perhaps the postman

holds the lift

and the safety pins

are where we last saw them

The Cottage

The memory built me around it.
An abandoned trail. A forest with no sky.
I was both the wood of the axe

and the wood of the tree.
A cat was dying in my bag,
and when the leaves looked away

I snuck it crushed berries from the path
and dead sparrows whose hearts
had burst out of their chests.

The scarlet stained my palm –
whether the blood of the berry or of the bird,
I couldn't tell.

I was thirsty but afraid to drink.
When I reached the cottage,
you were waiting. You led me inside.

I offered you my hand, which you licked.
It was cleaner then
than it had ever been before.

Then you placed my hand on the door,
told me to cure it.
The door disappeared beneath my hand.

Reader, I Married Him

A golden shovel after the song 'Midnight Train to Georgia',
performed by Gladys Knight & the Pips

If you asked me why I made myself so small, I'd
show you the river; the one that would rather
gorge itself on sewage than be clean. I'd give you a toe to live
upon, a rotten tree to kneel before, a dustpan to curl up in,
a name pried from a ghost. My laughter was thin, but his
gave all the birds a breath to glide on. Remedy for a wretched world.
I was never that attached to me anyway. Never more than
a ribbon's stretch away from curling against a blade. I once put a live
wire on my tongue to taste the void. It was not without
its sweetness. That sleep – like choking on feathers, like him:
the place where women went to die. The way he fucked me in
front of the mirror, so I'd know that the face beneath him was mine.

GMT–1

it's 10 p.m. here   9 there
I already know what you will did.

When it happens, you'll flooded your mouth
with vodka, burned away the taste.

At that moment, I was mercy-killing
the mouse with the poison you'll tell me to buy.

The fence collapsed, sensing
that the ground beneath it will shift.

In my mind, I saw her before you will:
the beachfront bar, the dancing flames,

the island coast shaped like
the crab that will abandoned its shell.

I watched her midnight-coloured hair
grow minute by minute towards her waist,

and the rash that will burst on your thighs
from an hour thrashing in cheap hotel sheets.

The text you will sent me right after confessed
about the toothpaste whose cap will stray.

And when I called, you will mumble.
Words will lost their way. I said *wait for you*

but you'll hear *weight for you* – and jetsam me
to the ocean widening between us.

From here, I saw your footsteps
on the path you'll swore you'd never tread.

The path I knew you will.

My mother calls

and asks me for a synonym for *regret.*

Disappointment? I say.

She says it's not quite right.

Remorse?

No.

Bitterness?

No.

Dissatisfaction? Grief?

None of them quite capture what she is trying to convey.

Regret? I suggest.

Yes, she breathes. Yes, exactly.

Your Mother's Daughter (a GIF)

you will be nothing / like your mother who hoarded / scabs on her knees praying
daily / for a boy, she gave everything / once was found hanging / wind chimes
drowning out / your cry desperate / you have a habit of breaking / your
mother's heart echoing fault lines / an invaded coast, you lost the more desirable
you became / out of reach, leaves fall / in the wrong order, as you were taught,
you bow, then you break / your silence destroying your mirror / your mother
teaching daughter how to feel for lumps / how to hold her own stomach in / to
stomach what she holds in / she umbilicals to you all / lifelong the sentence /
fraying when you trust yourself most / unlearn what you were taught / a fable
gleaned from crumpled receipts / tell your daughter you are inevitable / an
inescapable story / but /

you will be nothing like your mother / who hoarded
scabs on her knees / praying daily for a boy / she gave everything once / was
found hanging wind chimes / drowning out your cry / desperate / you have
a habit of breaking your mother's heart / echoing fault lines, an invaded coast /
you lost the more desirable you / became out of reach / leaves fall in the wrong
order / as you were taught, you bow / then you break your silence / destroying
your mirror, your mother / teaching daughter how to feel for lumps / how to
hold her own / stomach in to stomach / what she holds in, she umbilicals to you
/ all lifelong, the sentence fraying / when you trust yourself most, unlearn what
you were taught / a fable gleaned from crumpled receipts / tell your daughter
/ *you are inevitable, an inescapable story* / *but* /

Chaotic Good

Friend, that wasn't you last night at the cinema – the one with sticky floors and seats that smell like nachos and cum. You would never be caught dead there. You always said that your laugh became a shriek in the dark: people forget themselves when no one's looking. As for me, I notice more. You cross your ankles when you sit, even on the bus. As quiet as a boiler's hum, milk-sore and motherly. Faithful even to the ammonia in your cloth, peeling you back. And so I know it wasn't you at the cinema, in the lobby, wearing the bob wig I lent you. With one hand in the pocket of a man who is not your husband, the other wrapped around a long pink can of raspberry gin. Your cleavage spilling out of the blue dress that you fingered when we went shopping and called *so trashy* with a smirk. How could it have been you? The way he stood over you, his hand squeezing your waist as you threw back your head to laugh, his eyes plumbing the depths of your throat. How engorged your tongue must have been. How wet. How you never knew it could be. When we were thirteen, we saw a man fasten his girlfriend's seatbelt and you said, *I want to be loved just like that.* You followed every rule to its dead end, and became a monument to surrender. And so it couldn't have been you because you were at home, polishing your church shoes for the next day. You were oiling your scalp and ironing his briefs, trying not to picture the one who takes them off. Before bed, you called me and said we should walk together in the morning. You would wait for me by the spotless gate whose hinges are rusted shut. You would never take the shaded path, the one whose thorns reach for your skirt – even though you would come alive there. Even though you'd love the berries that would burst against your hands. That's how I know it wasn't you, and that's why, when I see you, don't worry, don't worry, I won't even bring it up.

The Maelstrom

And after in the kitchen, crouched like dogs abundant with shit,
we sweep shards of frosted glass into the dustpan's horrified mouth.
You would've caught the vase if you'd seen it was the wedding gift
from your ex. And I would've thrown it harder if I'd known
you wouldn't duck. Silence blisters, then it breaks. At our antipode
two currents collide. Twist each other in a dance they cannot quit.
Like an ocean, a marriage is only ever as powerful as it is deep.
Make me a fathom I cannot fathom. Humble me with the plum pits
I would've choked on if you hadn't cut them out. Even though
I am hard water, even though I trapped you in a cinema tip-up chair.
When we sleep, the pinwheel on the balcony spins both ways.
When the shower drain is clogged it means you are thinking
of choking me. How unapologetically a knife performs its duty.
And how dutifully I became the place for you to drown.

I'm Here/Gone (delete as appropriate)

We were a (miracle/curse). Like an iceberg breaking off
    separating a predator from its prey.

Like two feet squeezed in a single sock –
    our flesh cleaving (together/apart).

This morning, I saw two squirrels (dancing/fighting)
    over a wafer of bread, and I thought about

that (joke/threat) you made – the one about the spider
    who (worshipped/devoured) her mate after he fathered her child.

Or was it the (vision/nightmare) you buried in me?
    The one about the cat who let the mouse eat all his food

so she'd be too (happy/heavy) to run away.
    I forget whose (hopes/fears) we were

(loyal/chained) to. The first time you said my name,
    I imagined (resting/choking) on your beard,

falling into your (lap/accusations) and (watering/starving)
    my desires to make them (bloom/tame).

Your fingers tugging on my strands;
    I was (woven/riven) by your touch.

The eggshells to our omelettes saying:
    look at what we (made/broke).

If I (stay/leave) it's because I once saw my mother
    make paella from three days' worth of leftovers.

It's because I found a (diamond/compass)
  in the ash of the (veil/map) I burned.

It's being lost and lonely in your (absence/presence),
  my breath held until you (return/leave).

REBIRTH

The Butterfly Effect

A phenomenon in which a minute change in one context can have huge effects elsewhere

13	31
Am I root or stem? Changing	Changing stem or root? I am
ways: scarred and new in growing.	growing in new and scarred ways.
Remember	Remember
a tide carving its future. Your	your future, its carving tide. A
whole mind splintered,	splintered mind, whole.
rogue all summer. That and	And that summer: all rogue.
scorching Blackpool, and	And Blackpool scorching,
the donkey panting on heavy legs. My	my legs heavy on panting donkey, the
mother – watching waves,	waves watching Mother.
but drinks nothing.	Nothing drinks. But
Am I	I am
learning thirst?	thirst, learning.
My fatherly frown,	Frown fatherly, my
my remnant	remnant; my
of him in retrograde.	retrograde in him. Of
Course of coarse.	coarse, of course.
Reclaiming shells, gleaning	Gleaning shells, reclaiming
dust and bone. Armour discarded.	discarded armour – bone and dust.
Afterlife: twisting, surging. Am I	I am surging, twisting afterlife
my past?	past my
I regret hardening.	hardening regret. I
Nothing left	left nothing
behind.	behind.

Alicante

The city is perfect: I don't know a single person.
For days, the only words I say are *perdón* and *gracias*.

To waving palm trees and leafy plazas: *gracias*.
To Alhambra tiles and coloured steps: *gracias*.

To the crumbling castle on a high cliff. Halfway up,
I ask an old couple how far it is to the top.

When I look up the word they use
I learn that the Spanish word for *summit*

also sounds like the word for *chasm*. How narrow it is,
the gulf between daring to fall and learning to rise.

In the square, church bells gather the hours.
There are more ahead of me than I thought.

Cool air lingers in shaded alleyways:
under washing lines heavy with fresh linen;

on balconies whose voile curtains flap
against metal chairs like trapped wings.

Against all odds, my appetite returns.
Stuffed with lobster paella and rosé,

meatballs and rioja, fried potatoes, garlic prawns,
yet I make room for every souvenir I can bear.

The shopkeeper who reads me her son's poems.
The waiter who sings to me in Catalan.

The museum guide who points out a Neolithic axe
from a cave nearby.

An eternity of women who have learned to break things
without breaking themselves.

I follow their echoes downhill towards the shore,
my sandals slapping against hot pavement,

then jagged steps
then mosaic tiles

then golden sand.
Saltwater for a wound and so I go in all the way.

Only the ocean knows how much I deepen in it.
Only the tide could draw me out, could bring me back.

The Lost Sheep

I grew up in a silent house
but faith is noisy
faith sounds like scraping chairs
and rustling envelopes
feedback from a dented microphone
the laughter of women counting coins in the back room
the choir coordinator's squeaking shoes
mama joy scoffing at sister anne's puff puff

someone would shout *glory* whenever john 10:10 was read out
a guttural cry that juddered my soles

it was forty days and nights before I realised that the voice
was mine

there is a certain light that only shines on closed eyes
you feel its warmth on your second skin
and run towards it while standing still
my legs were strong then
I ran towards it many times
so quick that no one else could see
but it let me catch it   swallow it
it lit me from within

if this is your first time
     raise your hand   come forward
if you believe
     repeat after me   receive   go out   convert   raise up

you will be filled
(once you empty yourself)

this is how you make yourself
(smaller)

how to endure
(what you should not)

every service a deeper lesson
a new way to lessen

the heart prays differently to the mouth
may all wavering depart
a plea
not to remove   but to be removed

if this is your last time
don't tell a soul
leave quietly halfway through the message
out the back door that a dove once flew into
      broke itself against
      whether to join us or to die only god knows
refuse counsel for your stubborn feet
tear out the page with colossians 3:18 underlined
struggle to pray for two years after
forgetting how   wondering why

when a pastor stops you in the street
invites you back
tell him that the lost sheep wasn't lost
she was searching
and in that wilderness she found
not a burning bush but a smouldering weed
and its fire doesn't speak
but it keeps her warm
and most days that is enough

Dear Eve (a letter to his second wife)

What you have heard is true: the world was young once
and so was I. At the edge of the garden there was
only more garden, and a serpent shedding its obedience.
Who am I to judge? I drop things because
they aren't safe in my hands: mornings cracked
like eggs that spit and then harden in resignation;

the heart of a man who climbed trees as a boy
and still flinches at the snap of a branch. The first time
he mentioned you, he sucked the side of his thumb
and then hooked it in his jeans: *Good for food
and pleasing to the eyes.* I know you are the reason
he learned to text with his hand in his pocket;

why, whenever he came, he murmured *fuck* into the pillow,
bitch against my hair. He cursed everything
that wasn't you. By now, I bet he's led your hand
to the spot he calls his *rapture*. You know the one I mean.
I'm sure you've heard the sound he makes when
it's pressed. May your fingers find it on days that bite:

when another man squeezes your shoulder,
when his brother's plot yields more maize,
when the oxen look him in the eye. Put cocoa butter
on memories that crack. Crush bay leaves and mahogany bark
for the cock that wanders at night. Burn the hairs
of a coconut's scalp and your son will be nothing

like his father. A cracked mug for a libation cup.
Corn husk as catacomb. If in doubt, doubt everything.
Look both ways before you tell them your name.
Do you recoil at the thought? Do you hold my sins against me?
I was formed from dust, not rib –
should I be cursed for the ground I claim as mine?

I was pure once, now I am well. I choose the hard bed,
I choose the broken chair. I can't smell myself anymore.
My story has so many versions I forget which one is true:
The hiss called me, but I ran from it
No, I ran from the hiss but it called me back
No, I ran toward the hiss, not from it

Some thoughts get uglier the truer they become.

Sankofa

From the Akan proverb, 'Se wo were fi na wosankofa a yenkyi', meaning:
'It is not taboo to go back for what you left behind'

This time, I go back to save you (21) from yourself. We go out, and I watch
from the cab as you run barefoot through a fountain. In a spotless street, we find
a church winking in the dark, and a fisher of men reeling in folks for all-night
service. His smile tugs your insides. When he says he sees God in you, you burst
out laughing, sneakily drop the zoots tucked in your bra. Every hour on the hour
I nudge you, tap SOS on your Bible – but you have never needed morse code.

This time, I go back, tell you (28) to leave him. But you're more faithful to the code
of silence you keep than to your own soul. Even you can't bear to watch:
you cover your mirror with coats and mop away your footsteps every hour.
What can I say that you have not already ignored? I offer you a key but find
you stiff on a broken bed, hours from sleep, your bladder about to burst,
the freezer choked with frost, the leaky tap weeping quietly through the night.

This time, I go back because I know this is where it starts. You (7) hide all night
under covers, imagining sisterly cuddles and the secrets you two share in code.
On hot days, you press palms to pavement cracks, trap the ants trying to burst
through. Summer is mean and peels your clothes off. I give you a princess watch
and the two hands meet as you take mine. Safety feels like us. In the park, we find
a swing on your favourite tree, and I push you – higher and higher – for hours.

This time, I go back to help you (14) escape. Your parents argue for an hour
in the kitchen before you sneak out through the balcony, hoping the night
will be kinder than the day. We ride the bus all the way to the end, find
a boy chasing himself on a merry-go-round. He knows the code
to a mansion nearby, and after hours of whisky and jazz, we watch
the sun rise over the river, envying the current when it bursts.

This time, I go forward, seeking life; I hold your (42) knees as your waters burst.
Our daughter has a birthmark on her foot shaped like a tree. In that golden hour,
our heartbeats sync and time stretches like a womb. All night, we watch
her chest rise, and fall, and rise and rise again. All night
we nurse our own cure. You sing blessings into her ear – an ancestral code
being rewritten – and we weave a blanket from the strongest thread we can find.

This time, I go forward, help you (35) look at cottages for weeks before you find
one you like. Overnight, hoarfrost sharpens the trees. The pipes burst
and the plumber who comes is all heavy boots and eager hands. The code
to his phone is our birthday. The broom in your hand falls in his direction. An hour
later by the lake, our tangled limbs remember what it means to be alive. All night,
we are afraid someone will catch us, but the moon keeps watch.

This time and every time, I was the code I needed to find my way back.
If you watch closely, you'll see it – how daylight bursts from doubt.
And how destinies hinge on hours; a song like ours that made it through the night.

Parthenogenesis

In the beginning, I was given a set of instructions with no parts to assemble. The onus to do it right. Do what exactly? It didn't matter. I scoured the streets around town, salvaged shed hairs, a wooden button, a scrap of apron, an armrest from a sofa. I made a doll's house out of scrap wood, carved a doll and tied her to the bed.

Then one day I saw a chair tipping in the wind and I steadied it. I steadied it with my hand. In that moment, I realised what I was meant to build.

In the process, I found a photo of myself ten years in the future – my legs strong and womb stretched with promise, my hand skimming the hedge behind my house where my children play. In the process, I found friendship in new hands and old ones and young ones and strong ones and sore ones and small ones and big ones and all of them true enough to rest in. I grew wise watching a tree at dawn shuddering off its snow. Reminders to rub my scalp in sprigs of rosemary. Solace in the form of a cat sunning itself on a wall. Laughter in jasmine tea, botanic gardens, rum punch and amapiano, a dusty library's hidden stacks. Isn't this what I wanted? My mother peeling an apple in one strand. Meatballs nudged into a bowl. What gifts, that I didn't even hint about. And I colour-corrected them against my teeth, I never had to check the collar to see if they belonged to somebody else. If there is beauty, I became it once on frozen grass, watched by ducks and dying trees. I felt an urge where hope once lived and so I squatted in the mud, pushing against a crowning truth. And the waters that broke washed my feet, and the child who fell in my hands had my face – and no, I did not come easy, but I knew how to build myself up when I did.

Still Here

I guess the devil could've swallowed me
if I didn't have all this ass. I guess the foxes
in my garden – sniffing used tissues and bloodied pads –
would've dragged me through the bushes if my taste
didn't make them fear night.
Admit that a falcon diving through the air
reminds you of me. Or a heater turned all the way up.
Or a road that bends but doesn't break.
I burned all the bridges beneath my feet
and was so fly I didn't even get wet.
Not the ocean but the salt that seasons it.
Not your dog but the ball it can't catch.
And when my enemies lock the gates,
I'll go through the back door I carved with my teeth.
Call me vertebrae. Call me bedrock.
Call me Polaris for the lamb that's lost its way.
My forgiveness brings all the damned to the yard.
My fine print sings only their praise.
I sew gold into my weave, stir up fake friends
like morning brew: too frothed up. Semi-sinned.
Dividing lies by the truth I made,
charting my future
by the prophecy I became.

Notes

'The way you say *pen*' is written after Irène P. Mathieu's 'Soil'.

'Mamlambo, Marooned' is written after Vievee Francis's 'A Flight of Swiftlets Made Their Way in'. A mamlambo is a deity in Zulu mythology, often depicted as a large snake-like creature. It is known as the 'goddess of rivers', has the capacity to shape-shift, and is notorious for drowning its victims and then sucking out their brains.

'One side of a conversation with the bailiff at my door' is written after Hanif Abdurraqib's 'One Side of an Interview with the Ghost of Marvin Gaye'.

'Finding my dad in a can of baked beans' was inspired by the song 'Inkanyezi Nezazi (The Star and the Wiseman)', performed by Ladysmith Black Mambazo.

'The Redemption of Vanity' is written after an artwork of the same name by Diemut Strebe, in which a 16.78 carat yellow diamond (the most brilliant material on earth) is covered with carbon nanotubes that absorb 99.995% of all light (the blackest material on earth). When covered, the diamond appears to disappear.

The title of 'Burst me into song' is borrowed from a line in the poem 'The Virgin Speaks of What She Endured' by Shivanee Ramlochan.

The song 'Midnight Train to Georgia', which inspired 'Reader, I Married Him', was written by Jim Weatherly and performed by Gladys Knight and the Pips.

'GMT−1' is written after William Gee's 'tomorrow my brother died'.

'The Butterfly Effect' is written after Rita Dove's 'Mirror'.

In 'Dear Eve (a letter to his second wife)', the phrase 'What you have heard is true' is borrowed from Carolyn Forché's poem 'The Colonel'. The phrase '*Good for food / and pleasing to the eyes*' is borrowed from Genesis 3:6.

'Still Here' is written after Lucille Clifton's 'won't you celebrate with me' and Nikki Giovanni's 'Ego Tripping'.

Acknowledgements

Previous versions of some of these poems have appeared in the following publications: *a cough of pollen: Winchester Poetry Prize 2023 anthology* (Winchester Poetry Festival), *bath magg, Callaloo, Creative Writing Anthology 2022* (Aesthetica Magazine), *harana poetry, Lolwe, London Magazine, Oxford Poetry, Propel Magazine, Poetry Review* and *Wet Grain*.

Several poems previously appeared in *Ripe* (ignitionpress, 2020).

'Path of Least Resilience' won First Prize in the Winchester Poetry Prize 2023. 'Turkish Delight' won Second Prize in the London Magazine Poetry Prize 2022. 'Ahead Only' was shortlisted for the Aesthetica Creative Writing Award 2022. A version of 'Anti-Hero' was part of a portfolio which was shortlisted for the Brunel International African Poetry Prize 2021. Several of the poems in the 'P___Y' sequence were Highly Commended in the Manchester Poetry Prize 2023. Many thanks to the judges of these prizes.

Thank you to the tutors, administrators, classmates and/or collaborators at the following organisations where my craft has developed over the years: the Covent Garden Stanza, the Arvon Foundation, the London Library's Emerging Writers Programme, Writerz and Scribez, the Bridge, Spread the Word, the Poetry School, All Saints Sessions, the Obsidian Foundation and the MSt Creative Writing programme at Oxford.

Special thanks to Niall Munro and the entire team at ignitionpress for their unwavering support, and for first believing in me.

Many thanks to Anthony Anaxagorou for his incisive mentorship. To Wayne Holloway-Smith, Mary Jean Chan, Suna Afshan and Luke Allan for their attentive notes on some of these poems. To Helen Mort and George Szirtes for their prompts and encouraging words. To my fellow Foxgloves, Natalie Linh Bolderston, Maia Elsner, Tanatsei Gambura, S. K. Grout, Maryam Hessavi, Rowan Lyster, S. Niroshini, Warda Yassin and Fathima Zahra, as well as alice hiller and Patrick Romero McCafferty, for years of incredible chats, invaluable friendship and insightful feedback.

Love and thanks to Adenike Ojo for always being so understanding, and for always cheering me on. To Judith Hammond for a lifetime of laughter and support; so many of my childhood joys are because of you. To my mother and brother for their love, for painting my room when I couldn't, and for everything else.

I am so grateful to my agents, Veronica Goldstein and Sabhbh Curran, and to everyone at United Talent Agency and Curtis Brown, for helping these words find the right homes.

Thank you to the Society of Authors and the Authors' Foundation, whose support made this book possible. To the teams at *Magma*, *Poetry London*, *Poetry Wales*, *Tentacular* and the Ledbury Poetry Critics programme, for creating spaces for me to explore what poetry is and what it can be.

Deepest thanks to the entire team at Faber & Faber (past and present) for all their kindness, dedication and creativity – especially Matthew Hollis for believing in the collection, Lavinia Greenlaw for helping it come to life with so much care, and Lavinia Singer, Jane Feaver and Hazel Thompson for making me feel so welcome. Big thanks also to Suzanna Tamminen and the team at Wesleyan University Press for embracing my book and me with so much warmth.